Catholic
SAINTS
for
CHILDREN

Under the direction of Romain Lizé, Vice President, MAGNIFICAT

Editor, MAGNIFICAT: Isabelle Galmiche
Editor, Ignatius: Vivian Dudro
Proofreader: Anne Dabb
Assistant to the Editor: Pascale van de Walle
Layout Designer: Elena Germain
Production: Thierry Dubus, Sabine Marioni

Original French edition: *Les saints de ma communion*
© 2015 by Mame, Paris
© 2015 by MAGNIFICAT, New York • Ignatius Press, San Francisco
All rights reserved.
ISBN Ignatius Press 978-1-62164-041-7 • ISBN MAGNIFICAT 978-1-941709-04-7

Catholic
SAINTS
for
CHILDREN

Texts by
Emmanuelle Heme

Illustrations by
Elvine

Translated by Janet Chevrier

MAGNIFICAT · Ignatius

CONTENTS

Saint Mary, Mother of Jesus

May it be done to me according to your word.

Mary was a young woman of Nazareth awaiting the coming of the Messiah. While she was betrothed to Joseph, the carpenter, she was visited by an angel who announced to her that she was to give birth to the Savior, the Son of God! How was that possible? The angel explained to her that the Holy Spirit would come upon her with the power of God. And Mary agreed. She said yes. And that *Yes* was to change the whole world! Mary gave birth to Jesus. She loved Jesus and watched over him as he grew up until, one day, she let him go off to do the will of his Father in heaven. She always trusted in God: when the angel appeared to her, when Jesus spoke of amazing things. . . and even at the foot of the cross.

Mary holds a special place in heaven close to her Son, Jesus. He gave her to us all as our Mother. You can confide anything to her; she will share it with Jesus and teach you, too, to trust in the Lord.

Prayer

Hail Mary, full of grace,
the Lord is with thee.
Blessed art thou among women,
and blessed is the fruit of thy womb, Jesus.

Holy Mary, Mother of God,
pray for us sinners,
now, and at the hour of our death.

Amen.

Saint Joseph

Joseph, son of David, do not fear to take Mary into your home.

Joseph was a carpenter who lived in the little town of Nazareth. He was of the house of David, a descendant of the greatest king of Israel! Joseph was betrothed to Mary. But, one day, he learned that Mary was going to have a baby, even though they were not yet living together. He decided to let Mary go quietly, but that night, the angel of the Lord spoke to Joseph in a dream. The angel told him to have no fear to take Mary into his home, because the baby she was expecting was from God. Joseph trusted in the Lord: he welcomed Mary, and when she gave birth to a son, Joseph named him Jesus and cared for him as his own son. He helped him to grow up and taught him the carpenter's trade.

Saint Joseph teaches us to trust in God with all our heart, even in what might seem to be a tricky situation. He was the foster father of Jesus. You can ask him to protect your own daddy, to bless his work, and to guide him.

Prayer

Joseph, you are called the Just, the Silent One.
I want to call you my friend.
With Jesus and Mary, you have a place in my heart,
you are part of my life.

You, who welcomed the Lord into your home,
help me to find him.
Tell me where he is when I am fearful and lonely.
Tell me where he is when I am full of courage,
and others come to me for friendship and joy!

Joseph, my friend,
teach me to meet the Lord each day;
you, who witnessed the action of the Holy Spirit,
help me to recognize his wonders.

You, who took such good care of your own family,
keep my heart and my hands wide open.

(Adapted from a poem by Bishop Léon Soulier)

Saint Peter

Jesus asked them, "But who do you say that I am?" Peter answered him, "You are the Christ."

You know who Peter is: he was one of Jesus' twelve Apostles. His first name was Simon. He was a fisherman who left everything, including his home and his relatives, to follow Jesus. Simon lived alongside Jesus, listened to him, and saw everthing he did. He was sure of one thing: he would follow Jesus to the death; he would never abandon him! He understood that Jesus was the long-awaited Messiah, the Christ. That is why Jesus gave him the name Peter, which means "rock." Jesus said to him: "You are Peter, and on this rock I will build my Church." And yet, when Jesus was arrested and condemned to death, Peter was frightened and denied he even knew Jesus! Peter betrayed his best friend. But on Easter morning, he was one of the first Apostles to believe in the Resurrection of Jesus. He ran quickly to the tomb: it was empty! When they met again, Jesus asked him, "Peter, do you love me?" And Peter answered, "Yes, Lord, I love you." Peter knew he was forgiven. After Pentecost, he proclaimed the wonders of the Lord all the way to Rome, where he was the first pope and died a martyr, crucified like Jesus.

You can ask Saint Peter to give you his fervent love of Jesus, and to help you to welcome the tender gaze of Jesus, who forgives beyond all our expectations.

Prayer

You, Peter, who left everything to follow Jesus,
give me a heart as open as yours.

You, Peter, who recognized Jesus as the living
    Son of God,
give me a faith as clear and strong as yours.

You, Peter, who wept after denying your Lord,
grant that I may cry over my sins.

You, Peter, whom Jesus chose to lead his flock,
grant that I may pray for the pope, the bishops,
    and the priests
whom the Lord gives us today.

It was you whom Jesus asked three times,
    "Peter, do you love me?"
Like you, I want to answer today,
"Lord, you know everything. You know that I love you!"

Saint Paul

If I do not have love, I am like a clanging cymbal.

Saul did not believe that Jesus was the Savior and persecuted those who did. When Saint Stephen was stoned, he was there—and said nothing! But one day, on his way to the city of Damascus to arrest Christians, he was thrown to the ground. He heard a voice say to him, "Saul, why are you persecuting me?" Saul asked, "Who are you, Lord?" The voice answered, "I am Jesus, the one you are persecuting." When Saul got to his feet, he was blind. His life turned upside-down. His heart changed. Scales seemed to fall from his eyes. He took the name Paul and soon became a great missionary, moved by the fire of the Holy Spirit that filled him with strength and daring. He traveled throughout many Mediterranean countries making known the name of Jesus. Many people came to him and believed in Jesus—but he also made many enemies and was often thrown in prison for his preaching. He wrote many letters to all the new Christians he had visited, guiding and encouraging them.

Ask Saint Paul to give you the right words to speak of your faith and the courage to live according to the words of Jesus, with forgiveness and kindness. Your actions will speak louder than words!

Meditation

If I have all faith
so as to move mountains,
but do not have love, I am nothing.

If I give away everything I own to feed the hungry,
if I hand my body over to be burned,
but do not have love, I gain nothing.

Love is patient, love is kind.
Love is not jealous or boastful;
it is not arrogant or rude.
Love does not insist on its own way;
it is not irritable or resentful;
it does not rejoice at wrong,
but rejoices in the right.
Love bears all things, hopes all things,
endures all things.

Love never ends.

(See 1 Corinthians 13:2–8)

Saint Augustine

You have made us for yourself, Lord, and our hearts are restless until they rest in you!

Augustine was born in North Africa in the fourth century. His father, who was not a believer, was very strict. Augustine had a solid education and learned Greek philosophy. His mother, Monica, a Christian, prayed devoutly for her son who, though a good student, loved having fun and enjoying himself better than anything. For a long time, he passionately sought the meaning of life. He wanted to see everything, try anything! But one day, he discovered that the truth he had been seeking so hard was the infinitely great God of the Christians, who dwelled within his own heart! Augustine became passionate about Jesus! He sought knowledge and understanding to help belief. After his death, the Church proclaimed him a Doctor of the Church, which means that his writings can help other Christians to deepen their faith.

You can pray to Saint Augustine for God to put on your path people, places, and good books that will nourish and enliven your faith.

Meditation

Love and do what you will.

If you keep silent, keep silent by love.
If you speak, speak by love.
If you correct, correct by love.
If you pardon, pardon by love.

Let love be rooted in you,
and from that root nothing but good can grow.

(Adapted from a homily by Saint Augustine)

Saint Genevieve

We women will go on praying to God until he hears our pleas.

Saint Genevieve lived in Paris in the fifth century. She is often depicted as a young girl with long hair. At the age of seven, she offered her life to the Lord: she would not marry but would give all her time to the service of the poor and the sick. She was brave and deeply committed to peace. One day, the Huns, led by their chief, Attila, arrived from Turkey and tried to invade Paris. Genevieve, though only twenty-eight, succeeded through her strength of character in persuading the Parisians to pray, to resist, and never to abandon their city to the invaders. And that was how Genevieve managed to avoid war. She became the patron saint of Paris.

Saint Genevieve drew all her strength from God: when you are faced with hardship, she can teach you her courage and strength of will. Ask her, who preferred words rather than weapons, to protect the peace and to help you to avoid fighting.

Prayer for peace

O my God, our Father,
you give us everything.

From you comes light, life, love;
from you comes peace.

O Father, give us peace.

Give peace to our world.
Give peace to hearts that are closed.
Give peace to peoples at war with each other.

Give peace to broken families.

O Father, give us peace through your Son,
Christ, the Prince of Peace.
Help us to welcome your peace,
and to be builders of peace.

Amen.

Saint Benedict

What, most dear brethren, could be more sweet to us than the voice of the Lord inviting us?

Benedict was born in the fifth century near Rome, where he was sent for his education. But he fled this noisy city of endless partying in search of a "desert" where he could live with God and become a hermit. Monks from a nearby abbey begged him to become their abbot. He accepted, but the monks, annoyed at his attempts to correct their bad habits, tried to poison him! Having unmasked the plot, Benedict left them and returned to his grotto. It was then that other men joined him, seeking to live with him according to the Gospel. Benedict, whose faith worked miracles, founded several monasteries and wrote a text, called the Rule of Saint Benedict, to organize the lives of monks. Still the guide for many abbeys today, it is based on two simple instructions: *ora et labora* ("pray and work").

You can pray to Saint Benedict for all monks and religious, and ask him to guide you to love those around you, and to lead a simple, beautiful life. Benedict's first piece of advice: "Put nothing, absolutely nothing, before Christ."

Prayer

Saint Benedict,
you who were a great master
in the school of divine service,
grant that, putting nothing before love of God,
we may hasten with a loving heart
in the way of his commands.

Lord,
through the wisdom of Saint Benedict
you drew many souls to you.
Protect all those who wish to serve
in the monastic life.

Grant that we may run to you with a joyful heart,
with the sweet taste of peace and the strength of
faith.

Amen.

(Based on prayers from masses for Saint Benedict)

Saint Hildegard of Bingen

God created man like a wonderful precious gem.

Saint Hildegard, who lived in Germany, was a courageous woman of the Middle Ages. She was a mystic, which means she lived in such deep union with God that it sometimes produced extraordinary results: from the age of three, she experienced visions! And she became a Benedictine nun at the young age of sixteen. She delighted to find in nature everything needed for men and women to live in health and harmony with each other. She developed many talents: she was simultaneously a doctor, a musician, and a theologian! She invented remedies and recipes, and gave advice about a healthy diet— what a very learned woman!

Saint Hildegard can teach you the wonder of all creation, how to protect nature, and to care for your own body, as well. She can help you to develop the talents you have been given so that they may blossom for you and for others.

Prayer

Bless the Lord,
all you works of the Lord!

You heavens, bless the Lord;
sun and moon, stars of heaven, rain and dew,
bless the Lord!

All you winds, bless the Lord.
Fire and heat, frost, cold and ice and snow,
bless the Lord!

Mountains and hills, seas and rivers, bless the Lord!

Plants, animals, birds of the air, bless the Lord.
Fish of the seas, oceans, and rivers, bless the Lord!

You children of men, bless the Lord;
praise and exalt him above all forever.

(See the Book of Daniel 3:57–87)

Saint Dominic

Let us go forward in joy, thinking of our Savior!

Dominic was a Spanish priest with special concern for the poor and the spread of the Gospel. For Dominic, these two things went hand in hand! And so, when famine struck, he sold his precious books to feed the hungry. In the thirteenth century, certain Christians in the south of France, the Cathars, separated from the faith of the Church and made up their own religion. For example, they insisted that Jesus was never really a man, and they did not believe in the Resurrection. Deeply troubled by this, Dominic founded the Order of Preachers, men who, like the Apostles, set out on the road two by two to preach the Gospel.

Gifted with great intelligence, Saint Dominic spread the faith through his words and writings. You can pray to him to inspire you to tell others about Jesus with words that speak good and actions that do good. If you have an inquisitive mind, you can pray to him for knowledge and wisdom.

Prayer

Saint Dominic,
you who are a light of the Church,
you whom we call Master of Truth,
make ardent faith grow in me.

Help me
to search first of all for truth.

Grant me
the wisdom to keep in my heart
the Word of God, like a treasure,
the intelligence to better understand the teachings
   of the Church,
and a kind heart, always open to welcome others.

Fill me
with your burning love of God and others,
that I may have the courage to speak simply
   of the love of God
and to spread the Good News of Jesus to those
   around me.

Amen.

Saint Francis of Assisi

Be praised, my Lord, through all your creatures, especially through my lord Brother Sun, who brings the day; and you give light through him.

Francis was born in Assisi, Italy. How he loved singing and dancing and poetry. You could never get bored when he was around! Francis dreamed of becoming a knight. But he was captured in battle. After his release, he fell gravely ill and began thinking about the meaning of life. He had a change of heart. One day, as he was praying, he heard Jesus say to him: "Help me to rebuild my church." Francis immediately set to rebuilding the chapel of San Damiano, which was in ruins. His wealthy father was furious and threw him out. So Francis renounced his family fortune and set off on the roads proclaiming the words of Jesus: "Go, and everywhere proclaim that the Kingdom of God is near. Take no money, nor bag, nor shoes, nor walking stick." Francis proclaimed the Gospel to the sick and to rich and poor alike. Soon he had many followers. He loved nature with all his heart and knew how to speak to all creatures.

Saint Francis can help you to wonder at simple things: a beautiful landscape, a flower, a smile, or even a friend who comes to visit and lights up your day.

Prayer

Lord, make me an instrument of your peace.

Where there is hatred, let me sow love;
where there is injury, pardon;
where there is discord, harmony;
where there is error, truth;
where there is doubt, faith;
where there is despair, hope;
where there is darkness, light;
and where there is sadness, joy.

Lord, grant that I may not so much seek
to be consoled as to console;
to be understood as to understand;
to be loved as to love.
For it is in giving that we receive;
it is in pardoning that we are pardoned;
and it is in dying that we are born to eternal life.

Amen.

Saint Louis, King of France

God gave me everything. What I distribute in alms is well spent.

Louis IX was king of France. He was a just and honest man. With his wife, Marguerite, whom he loved dearly, he had eleven children. Louis' most cherished wish was to govern his kingdom according to the laws of God. Seated under an oak tree, he would render justice, listening to all his subjects equally, be they knights or peasants! Louis had a deep love of God and founded monasteries and hospitals. As a young man, he would disguise himself and go out in the streets giving alms to the poor. He was especially attentive to the most vulnerable. He kept the peace in his own country and went on crusade to defend Christians in the Holy Land.

Pray to Saint Louis to teach you to love your country, to be fair, and to listen to your heart. It will tell you what is right and good. Saint Louis will give you the courage to be faithful, to be honest, to be a peacemaker, and to love justice.

Prayer

Saint Louis, King of France,
you who were a devoted king to the people entrusted
    to you,
teach me to be someone people can trust.

You who defended peace,
teach me always to prefer forgiveness rather than quarrels,
and to create love around me—in my family and among
    my friends.

Saint Louis, King of France,
you who took Christ, Prince of the Poor, as your model,
you who, like him, were gentle and humble,
teach me to imitate Jesus, the King of my heart.

Amen.

Saint Rita

Peace I leave with you; my peace I give to you.

Rita lived in Italy. She wanted to become a nun, but, against her wishes, her parents married her at a young age to a rich and cruel man. Through gentleness and patience, Rita managed to improve her husband's character, though he remained short-tempered and made enemies. One day, he was murdered in an argument, and his two sons promised revenge! Rita prayed to God with all her might to stop her sons from becoming murderers. She would rather see them die than commit an evil act. In the end, Rita's sons begged her forgiveness for their vengeful plots before they died of the plague. Left all alone, Rita decided to enter the Augustinian monastery in her hometown of Cascia, just as she had always wished. The community agreed to accept her on condition that she make peace between her family and her husband's murderers. And Rita succeeded!

Rita faced great trials, but, through her gentleness and patience, peace prevailed. You can ask her to intercede in what may seem an impossible situation. She can also help you to forgive someone who has hurt you.

Prayer

Lord, you are my rock, my fortress, and my deliverer,
my rock, in whom I take refuge, my shield, my stronghold.
My Savior, you save me from violence.
In my distress, I called upon you.
You heard my voice; my cry came to your ears.
You reached from on high
and delivered me, because you love me.

Saint Rita, in your anguish, you turned to the Lord.
Like you, we entrust our trials, our pain, our hopes
to our Father in heaven and his Son Jesus.
Give us the courage and patience to overcome our
    sufferings.

Help us, Saint Rita, to say, like you, the words of Jesus:
"Father, may your will, not mine, be done!"

(Adapted from 2 Samuel 22:1–51 and a prayer to Saint Rita)

Saint Catherine of Siena

Conquer with the weapons of gentleness, love, and peace, rather than harshness and war.

Catherine's great dream was to consecrate herself to God, but she had to convince her parents first: to show them her commitment, she cut off her long hair! Her parents gave in, and Catherine was allowed to become a Dominican. She went about visiting and caring for the poor and the sick. She learned to read and many other things. But for Catherine, contemplating Jesus was better than any book! She believed we must allow Jesus to settle in our hearts as though welcoming him into a room; that is how to become an "other Christ." She became known everywhere for her love of Jesus. During the final years of the Middle Ages, many cities were at war against the pope, who fled to Avignon, France, for refuge. Wishing to restore peace, Catherine wrote to the great lords and sought out the pope to bring him back to Rome. Until her death, she traveled and wrote to safeguard the unity of the Church. For her great wisdom, she has been named a Doctor of the Church.

Saint Catherine watches over the pope, the Church, Europe, and leaders of all countries, that they may protect peace. May peace begin first within your own heart and in your family. Catherine can help you to love—even your enemies—just as Jesus loves us.

Prayer

O might of the Father, come to my aid!
Wisdom of the Son, enlighten my mind!
Sweet goodness of the Holy Spirit, burn within me!
My God, unite my heart with yours.

O eternal Father, I believe in your almighty power,
capable of rescuing the Church and delivering us
    from evil.

I believe in the wisdom of your Son,
which can enlighten my mind and that of your people
to help us to discern light from darkness.

I believe in the sweet goodness of your Holy Spirit,
whose fire can set my heart ablaze with charity.

Lord, establish peace in the world,
keep your Church united in love.
Come, Lord, never let my love for you slumber.

Amen.

(Based on a prayer of Saint Catherine to the Trinity)

Saint Joan of Arc

My Lord God, first served!

Joan lived in a village in the east of France. She helped her mother with the housekeeping. This was the time, in the fifteenth century, of the Hundred Years' War between the French and the English. France was overrun with English troops, and famine gripped the land. One day in the countryside, Joan heard the voices of the archangel Michael, Saint Catherine, and Saint Marguerite. They asked her to rout the enemy from the kingdom. Why her, a peasant girl, instead of a valiant knight? But Joan agreed, and the future King Charles VII granted her an army! She put on armor and led the French soldiers who ousted the English from the city of Orléans. Under her leadership, the French won great battles and helped Charles VII regain the throne of France—but she was taken prisoner by the allies of the English. They tried to make her say the voices she had heard were just a dream, but Joan would not lie! Falsely condemned for witchcraft, she was burned alive at the stake.

Saint Joan watches over all those who defend their country and its citizens. She can help you to keep your eyes and ears wide open to hear the call of peace from God.

Prayer

Saint Joan of Arc,
you who kept your trust in God
despite the battles and the lies,
help our country to grow in peace,
help us to fight evil
and stand fast in the love of Jesus.

Lord,
help my country to set an example,
keep us free from the prison
of our own failings.

Make us witnesses,
our feet shod in readiness to proclaim peace,
bearing in our hands the shield of faith,
and the sword of the Spirit, which is the word of God,
and wearing the helmet of salvation.

Give us the courage that comes from truth and justice,
and we will be victorious.

Amen.

(Based on Ephesians 6:14–17)

Saint Ignatius of Loyola

Neither want nor seek any other thing except, in all and through all, the greater praise and glory of God.

Ignatius was the youngest of thirteen children born to a noble Spanish family. He dreamed of fame through great feats of war. But during one battle, he was badly wounded in the leg. During his convalescence, having devoured every book of knightly romance in the library, he reluctantly decided to read the lives of the saints! In them, he gradually discovered that one could be heroic even outside the battlefield. The path he must take was the service of the Lord! He understood that our hearts need exercise in the love of Christ in order to live as one of his companions. He founded the Society of Jesus—the Jesuits—the order to which Pope Francis belongs. He understood that it is in turning to God that we can stop thinking only of ourselves and make the right choices.

Saint Ignatius can guide you when you need to make an important decision. He can help you to be discerning, to see more clearly in order to make the right choice.

Prayer

Lord, teach me to be generous.
Teach me to serve you as you deserve;
to give and not to count the cost,
to fight and not to heed the wounds,
to toil, and not to seek for rest,
to labor, and not to ask for reward,
except to know that I am doing your will.

(A prayer of Saint Ignatius)

Saint Teresa of Ávila

What a marvelous thing, that he who would fill a thousand worlds with his grandeur should enclose himself in something so small as us!

Teresa grew up in Ávila, Spain. She was the third in a family of twelve children! Even as a little girl, Teresa had an adventurous spirit. She planned to run away with her brother Rodrigo to convert the Moors and to die a martyr's death! But her father stopped her and so she decided to become a hermit and beg for food! As a young woman, Teresa tried to be popular. She became fashionable and flirtatious, but that did not make her happy. She went for a short stay in a convent where she suffered badly from the lack of freedom. She fell ill, but still she decided to persevere, for she had discovered how much she longed to unite herself totally with God. Saint Teresa became a great mystic: she had visions of Christ on the cross, which helped her to turn to Jesus. Because of her writings about the soul's journey to God, she is a Doctor of the Church.

You can ask Saint Teresa to help you to pray regularly, to learn how to be silent, and to welcome God into the castle of your heart.

Meditation

Let nothing trouble you,
let nothing frighten you.

All things are passing; God never changes.
Patience obtains all things.

He who possesses God lacks nothing:
God alone suffices.

(Saint Teresa of Ávila)

Saint Philip Neri

I will have no sadness in my house!

As a young boy, Philip liked visiting the Dominican Friars in the convent of San Marco in Florence, Italy. His faith grew as he contemplated the beauty of the frescoes painted there by Fra Angelico. At sixteen, he left his hometown for Rome to work in his uncle's business. But Philip soon found he preferred visiting the sick in the hospitals. One day as he was praying, he felt the fire of the Holy Spirit within him: he could feel his heart racing. He became a most joyful priest, but he sometimes became so lost in contemplation of Jesus while saying Mass, he had to have his cat playing at his feet to keep him attentive! The sick flocked to him, for he worked miracles. But he also tended the sick at heart, and spent much of his time in the confessional. He spoke about Jesus naturally, and many young people were drawn to follow him, so great was his lively faith and sense of humor. He also founded the Oratory, a group of priests living together, who sang, prayed, and visited the poor.

You can ask Saint Philip Neri to share with you his joy that comes from God, and to help you to laugh, to be ever cheerful, and to communicate your joy to those around you!

Prayer

Fill me with your joy!

Holy Spirit, breathe on me,
fill me with your joy,
that my heart may delight
because God loves me!

This joy that comes from God,
who can take it from me? Who can separate me from it?

Holy Spirit, let your fire shine in me,
let it warm the hearts of those I love:
my family, my friends, and all those I meet!

Saint Philip Neri, you who were joyful,
always cheerful, and full of hope,
help me to remain in joy,
in good times or bad!

Amen.

Saint Vincent de Paul

What! To be a Christian and see your brother afflicted without crying with him! That is to be a mere caricature of a Christian.

Vincent was a shepherd. His parents were humble farmers. One day, his father sent him away for his education. Seeing his ability, a family friend asked Vincent to become his children's teacher. Vincent discovered that he enjoyed teaching and speaking about Jesus and so he became a priest. Soon, the pope appointed him chaplain to the queen of France. She donated a large part of her fortune to the poor, and Monsieur Vincent, as he was known, was tireless on their behalf; he could never do enough for the needy. To help him in his work, he founded congregations such as the Daughters of Charity. His generosity was contagious: he was a friend to all, rich or poor, prisoners or orphans. He had immense trust in God. "First be generous," he said, "and God will do the rest!"

For Saint Vincent de Paul, every person is worthy of attention, of being listened to and loved. Ask him to help you to find a way to be of service to others, as far as your age and opportunities allow.

Prayer

Saint Vincent de Paul,
witness of Christ's charity to the poor,
give me a tender, compassionate heart
for the hardships and suffering of the most
    needy of the world.

Accompany me in the service I do,
and pray for me to the Son of God,
that I may become,
in my family, my neighborhood, my parish,
a fervent witness to his Gospel of Love.

Amen.

(Based on Saint Vincent de Paul's "cradle" prayer)

Saint John Baptist de La Salle

Show that you love those God has entrusted to you, as Jesus loved his Church.

John Baptist de La Salle lived in the town of Reims, France, during the reign of King Louis XIV. When he was very young, he wanted to become a priest. But his parents died and John Baptist had to take care of his six little brothers and sisters. What should he do? Give up his vocation? With the support of a priest, he persevered with his studies and became a priest at the age of twenty-seven. He devoted all his energy to improving schools. To do so, he founded an institute for teachers, the Brothers of the Christian Schools. There, brothers trained to become teachers in the schools established by John Baptist— free, well-organized schools for the poor (where children learned first of all to read in their mother tongue, instead of Latin, as rich children did); schools for grown-ups; and schools to learn a trade. He was full of ideas, especially the idea of teaching in a class, with one schoolteacher for several students, something new at the time!

You can ask Saint John Baptist to give you a generous heart and lots of ideas to share your knowledge with enthusiasm, and the courage to work well at school. You can also pray to him for your teachers!

Prayer

Lord,
thank you for giving us the chance to go to school,
to learn, to understand, to think.

Teach us to respect one another,
to listen to one another, to help one another.
Help us to make peace,
to avoid arguments and words that wound
in the classroom and on the playground.

Grant us the desire to work with confidence
and to progress with courage.
Give us your love and your wisdom
so that everyone may feel loved and listened to.

We pray to you for our teachers and our principal,
and for everyone who works in our school.

Amen.

Saint Kateri Tekakwitha

Who will teach me what is most pleasing to God, that I may do it?

Kateri was born in upstate New York in the seventeenth century. Her parents were a Mohawk chief and a Christian Algonquin woman. As a little girl, Kateri's whole family died of a terrible disease—smallpox. She alone survived, but her face was badly scarred and she was left almost blind. Her aunt and uncle adopted her and later tried to force her to marry. But Kateri refused: she consecrated her life to God and remained single. After that, she was treated like a slave. Kateri managed to find refuge with Jesuit priests and was baptized at the age of twenty. She established a community of Christian Native Americans who prayed together and cared for the sick. She died at the very young age of twenty-four, after a life full of trials.

Brave Kateri was ready to face any danger for her faith, and she wasn't afraid of making enemies. You can ask her to help you to say you are a Christian without fear and to live according to the Gospel.

Prayer

O Great Spirit,
whose voice I hear in the winds,
and whose breath gives life to all the world, hear me!
I am small and weak,
I need your strength and your wisdom.

Make me always ready to come to you
with clean hands and straight eyes.
So when life fades,
as the fading sunset,
my spirit may come to you.

Amen.

(Based on a prayer to Saint Kateri)

Saint John Mary Vianney

If when I die, I find that God does not exist, I will have been well-fooled. But I would still not regret having spent my life believing in love.

John Mary Vianney grew up at the time of the French Revolution: priests were persecuted and Mass was celebrated in the dark of night. He made his First Holy Communion at one of these secret Masses, and already he wished to become a priest. But his father was against it, as he needed him to work in the fields! At last, at the age of twenty, John succeeded in entering the seminary. The studies were long and difficult. And John struggled with Latin—a requirement to become a priest. But, finally, John became the curate of the village of Ars. He knew how to read into the depths of hearts. He prayed a great deal before the Blessed Sacrament, and his face shone with goodness. Crowds soon began arriving from all over to meet this "holy curé of Ars"—so much so that, by the end of his life, he was hearing confession from morning to night with hardly a moment of sleep!

Saint John Mary Vianney became the patron saint of priests. He is a role model for all boys who wish to become priests. Ask him to help you to be faithful in prayer, to respond to the call of the Lord, to find the words to touch the heart, and to comfort a friend in pain.

Prayer

I love you, O my God,
and my only desire is to love you
until the last breath of my life.

I love you, O my God,
and I would rather die loving you,
than live without loving you.

I love you, O my God,
and I want my heart to repeat it to you
with every breath I draw.

I love you, O my God,
and I ask that my love for you ever grows.

Amen.

(Based on a prayer of the Curé of Ars)

Blessed Frédéric Ozanam

The happiness of heaven is love! So let us not be afraid of loving too much!

Frédéric was born in the early nineteenth century, a time when many people were rejecting the Catholic Faith, and attacking priests and the teachings of the Church. For the sixteen-year-old Frédéric, it was difficult to believe. His philosophy teacher helped him to discover the love of God. And once he had, Frédéric decided to place himself in the service of truth, in his words and in his deeds. Gifted with great intelligence, Frédéric studied law, languages, and the Bible, and he became a university professor. But he didn't spend all day with his nose in books! His love of God gave him a wide-open heart that drew him toward others. He founded the Saint Vincent de Paul Society to train people and to send them out visiting the poor. Frédéric married and, until his death, he and his wife remained attentive to the needs of all those they encountered, no matter who they were.

Frédéric can help you to hear the simplest of calls from God: to do a good deed, to make someone smile, to give up a little of your time, to welcome a new student, and so on.

Prayer

Lord, my heart thirsts for you.

Help me to respond to your calls.
Give me friends to teach me how to love.
Help me to be worthy of them.

Place in my path people to guide me to you:
may they draw me to what is above, and not drag me down;
may they be generous, for I sometimes lack courage;
may they love you very much, for I am sometimes
    lukewarm toward you;
may they be kindly, that I may not be ashamed of
    my weaknesses.

Do not abandon me, Lord,
grant that I be loved and know how to love.
Give me the strength to fight for what is good,
    and for truth.

Amen.

(Based on a prayer of Frédéric Ozanam)

Saint John Bosco

I promised God I would give my life, to my last breath, for my poor boys.

John Bosco, a poor boy from Sardinia, spent his time looking for ideas to occupy the mischievous boys of his village. Later, he would create a youth club for young workers in the city of Turin, Italy. After school, boys could play sports, do other activities, and learn about God at this club. When John became a priest, he was still always there for the young. He took inspiration from the words of Saint Francis de Sales—"All in life is to be done through love and nothing by force"—to develop a model of education based on trust and love. That was how the young could grow, blossom, and become happy members of society.

Don Bosco, as he is known, can teach you to be attentive to others, to help everyone join in. You can pray to him for the children of the world who cannot go to school, for orphans, and for those who never get a chance to play. Don Bosco shows you must never give up hope in anyone, and that there is good to be found in every child!

Prayer

Saint John Bosco,
teach me to respect everyone and to share.
Teach me to play with everyone, and to be a good sport
on the playground and at home.

Saint John Bosco,
you who were ready to give your all for the young,
teach me to open my heart
to be attentive to others and to be of service.

Show me how I can be
a good role model to those younger than I am.

Amen.

Saint Bernadette

I have been told to tell you about it. I have not been told to make you believe it.

Bernadette was a poor girl from Lourdes, in the Pyrenees Mountains of France. One day, when she went to gather firewood at the grotto of Massabielle, she suddenly saw a lady in white standing in a cleft of the hillside. Bernadette returned several times, and each time the "beautiful Lady" spoke to her! At first, people thought Bernadette was crazy, that she was ill, and they made fun of her. But Bernadette stood firm. When miraculous water flowed from a spring the Lady told Bernadette to uncover, people began to believe her. Bernadette told her parish priest that the Lady wanted a chapel built. When she said the Lady's name was the Immaculate Conception, the priest realized that Bernadette was speaking about the Blessed Virgin! Since that day, crowds have flocked to Lourdes to pray to the Virgin Mary, to entrust their problems to her. Very many have been converted, and others, sick or handicapped, have washed in the waters of the spring and been cured. At twenty-two years old, Bernadette became a nun and remained in a convent until her death in 1879.

Saint Bernadette can teach you to have a simple heart, open to hearing what the Lord has to say to you. Ask her to teach you patience and gentleness. You can pray to her for anyone you know who is sick or suffering.

Prayer

O Virgin Mary,
Christians pray to you in Lourdes.
Ave Maria, hail to you, Mary.

In your sanctuary, refuge of sinners,
hear the cry of your children's hearts!
Ave Maria, hail to you Mary.

Like Bernadette, I pray
for the salvation of my brothers and sisters.
Ave Maria, hail to you, Mary.

In my heart, O Queen of Heaven,
replace hatred with charity.
Ave Maria, hail to you, Mary.

Tender mother, this is my desire:
to love you on earth and to see you in heaven!
Ave Maria, hail to you, Mary.

(Based on the Lourdes *Ave Maria*)

Blessed Charles de Foucauld

To pray is to think about God with love.

Charles was an army officer. He spent his time going to parties and having lots of fun. But one day, tired of his way of life, he went to a priest to make a confession, and his encounter with God was so overwhelming that he decided to devote his whole life to him. He became a priest and went to live in Nazareth, like Jesus, and then in the Sahara Desert. He became a hermit, which means he lived isolated from others, in a little shelter, and devoted all his time to prayer. He also went to meet the Touaregs, a nomadic people of the desert who did not share his religion. Charles did not try to convert them by words, but by his example, seeking only to be among them, to love them the way Jesus did. Perhaps that way they might discover God through him.

Charles loved all those the Lord placed on his path. You can ask him to give you his eyes to see in everyone, whatever his religion or the color of his skin, the mysterious presence of Jesus.

Prayer

Father,
I abandon myself into your hands;
do with me what you will.

Whatever you may do,
I thank you.

I am ready for all, I accept all.
Let only your will be done in me,
and in all your creatures.
I wish no more than this, O Lord.

Into your hands I commend my soul:
I offer it to you
with all the love of my heart,
for I love you, Lord,
and so need to give myself,
to surrender myself into your hands without reserve,
and with boundless confidence,
for you are my Father.

(Prayer of Brother Charles of Jesus)

Saint Thérèse, the Little Flower

To love is to give everything and to give oneself.

Thérèse was the youngest of a family of five girls. At the age of four, she lost her mother and became very delicate: she was often in tears and constantly craved attention. Her sister Pauline became her second mother. When Pauline entered a Carmelite convent, Thérèse was sick with sorrow, but she was miraculously healed. All her sisters became nuns, and Thérèse herself felt the call of God at a very young age. She wished to give her all to him. So, at fifteen, she entered Carmel. For her, what mattered was to do little things with great love. To be childlike, that was her secret! Thérèse accomplished no great feats in the convent, and yet, after her death, her love of Jesus touched thousands of hearts: she is a friend to all, even to those who are far from the faith!

Thérèse can help you to put love into the simplest of things: in your daily chores, as you enjoy a landscape, as you play, fix a meal, sing, help others, or just listen to a friend.

Prayer

My God, I offer you all my actions of this day.
I wish to sanctify each and every heartbeat,
every thought, every simple little action,
    by joining them to Jesus;
and I desire to make reparation for my sins
by casting them into the furnace of his merciful love.

O my God, for myself and for all my dear ones,
I implore the grace to fulfill perfectly your holy will
and to accept for love of you
all the joys and sorrows of this passing life,
so that one day we may be united in heaven
for all eternity.

Amen.

(Based on the prayer of Saint Thérèse)

Saint Maximilian Kolbe

Love never rests, but spreads like a consuming fire.

At the age of sixteen, Maximilian entered the Franciscans, monks who live in poverty like Saint Francis. He became a priest and went all the way to Japan, founding communities in honor of the Blessed Virgin. After his return home to Poland, the Second World War broke out: the Nazis sent Jews and those who resisted to concentration camps. Arrested and beaten, Father Kolbe was sent to Auschwitz. There he had to let go of his Franciscan robes for the prisoner's striped uniform. In the camp, he comforted and restored peace to those around him. One day, when several people were to be executed, Father Kolbe asked to die in place of the father of a family. He gave up his life for him, just as Jesus did for us.

Ask Saint Maximilian to help you to remain at peace when you go through difficult times. He often said: "Give yourself to others!" For him, that was the road to joy! Like him, you can entrust all the little details of your life to Mary.

Prayer

O Mary, Immaculate Virgin,
chosen among all women
to give birth to the Savior,
you who were the faithful servant of the Lord,
help us to answer the call of Jesus
and follow him on the path of life that leads to the Father.

Grant that our lives witness to the Gospel
in the midst of this world in search of the light.

O Mother of Jesus,
may all of creation join you
in praise of God for his mercy and infinite love.

Amen.

(Based on a prayer of Saint Maximilian Kolbe)

Blessed Pier Giorgio Frassati

For us, it is not permitted only to plod along; we must live!

Pier Giorgio was born to a large Italian family. He was an athletic young man, generous, enthusiastic, and full of fun. He was surrounded by friends with whom he loved to have laughs and go mountain climbing. He and his friends talked about God and how they could make the world around them a better place. *Verso l'alto* ("Upward!") was his motto. He often prayed and asked God to show him how he could be useful. He discovered the Saint Vincent de Paul Society and, in secret, visited the poor, fixed them meals, brought them medicine, and sometimes even his own coat! At twenty-four, he suddenly fell seriously ill. When he died only a few days later, his final thoughts were for the poor. On the day of his funeral, the church was filled to bursting: it was only then that Pier Giorgio's family realized all he had done to help others.

Pier Giorgio teaches us to be generous, attentive to others, and full of enthusiasm. You can ask him to help you to grow in great love of life, of Jesus, and of the poor.

Prayer

Pier Giorgio,
you who loved wide open spaces and the mountains,
you who feared no obstacle,
guide me on the path that leads *verso l'alto*!*

You who were funny and kind,
you who knew how to spread peace and joy,
show me how to draw others *verso l'alto*!

You who had an open and generous heart,
you who were a friend to all you met,
help my heart open up to God *verso l'alto*!

You who lived the joy of the Gospel,
you who always thirsted for God,
show me the path that leads *verso l'alto*!

Amen.

                                         * Upward!

Saint Teresa of Calcutta

We will never know all the good a simple smile can do.

At the age of eighteen, Agnes Bojaxhiu decided to become a missionary. She left Macedonia for Calcutta, India, where she became a schoolteacher. She whom we know as Mother Teresa was immediately shocked by the poverty she found there. One day while traveling and praying, she heard Jesus asking her, "Be my light, my fire of love; take me into the hovels of the poor, the homes of the sick and the dying; light the flame of my love." She obtained permission to live among the poor and to care for their sick and dying. Religious sisters joined her, and together they became the Missionaries of Charity. Famous the world over for her love of God and man, even Mother Teresa went through a period when she couldn't feel the presence of Jesus, when he seemed absent from her life, but she persevered.

Mother Teresa can help you to love God, and to go on serving him even when you feel discouraged, giving what you can, with joy: a smile, a kind look, a word of comfort. She said we must alway seek to do something beautiful for God.

Prayer

Mary, Mother of Jesus, give me your heart:
so beautiful, so pure, so immaculate;
your heart so full of love and humility,
that I may be able to receive Jesus in the Bread of Life
and love him as you love him,
and serve him in the distressing disguise
of the poorest of the poor.

(Based on the prayer of Mother Teresa)

Saint John Paul II

If you follow Christ, you will fully develop the potential within you.

Karol Wojtyła was from Poland. When he was young, he lost his mother, and then later his brother, too. He was brought up by his father, who was a devout Christian. When the Germans invaded Poland in World War II, his father fell ill and died. Karol found himself alone in the world. It was wartime, and his country was overrun first by the Nazi occupation and then by a Communist dictatorship. Karol became a priest, then a bishop, and fought for justice and peace. In 1978, he was elected pope and, until his death in 2005, he traveled the world, defending the family and the sanctity of life. He constantly repeated that life is sacred and that we must care for the most vulnerable among us, from the tiny baby in his mother's womb to the very elderly and sick. Pope Francis declared him a saint in 2014!

You can ask Saint John Paul II to give you the courage to defend the littlest and the most frail. He helps us to work for peace, starting within our own family. He teaches you to chase away fear to follow Jesus.

Prayer

O Mary, Mother of the living,
to you do we entrust the life of every person:
of little babies still in their mothers' wombs,
of all little children and families,
of the poor whose lives are made difficult,
of men and women who are victims of violence,
of those who, listening to your voice, work for peace,
of the elderly and the sick who are so frail.

Grant that all who believe in your Son, Jesus,
may proclaim the Gospel of Life.
Give them the courage to build,
together with all people of good will,
a world of truth and love,
to the praise and glory of God,
the Creator and Lover of Life.

(Based on a prayer of Saint John Paul II)

Printed in May 2024 by Dimograf, Poland
Job number MGN24L0613
Printed in compliance with the Consumer Protection Safety Act, 2008.